I DIED SO YOU DON'T HAVE TO

I DIED SO YOU DON'T HAVE TO

Starting, maintaining or just recognizing, your spiritual journey

By Chase

Copyright © 2023 by Chase Thomas

All rights reserved.

No portion of this book may be reproduced or used in any manner without the prior written permission of the copyright owner, except for the use of brief quotations.

Paperback ISBN: 979-8-218-16937-4

Written by Chase Thomas

Need a graphic designer? Reach out to Bryce Garcia

(twitter @uglydesigner)

Editing and proofreading by Debopriyo Dutta

(Twitter @debowrites)

Publishing by Indigo House Publishing

Table of Contents

1. Blame Yourself
2. Mental Housing
3. Identity
4. To Square One
5. What's Practice Without Equipment
6. Your Tools in Action
7. Failing is Necessary
8. Have to Maintain

Leaving Thoughts

Acknowledgement's

For, You.

PROLOGUE

As I sat in a lonely room in 2014, I never quite realized how much being yourself can help in every way possible. I also never understood why me, the person who took high school English the least bit serious, was called to write a book.

It goes to show that you have to trust the path the universe laid out for you and not get so caught up in the minuscule worries of things out of your control.

While I begin writing though, I am filled with a sense of possibility and hope. I'm ecstatic to document my journey so far and hopefully inspire you to start yours, or even help you maintain if you have already started.

Enjoy, friend.

1
BLAME YOURSELF

If you've picked this book up out of your own volition, I can maybe predict a few things about you – it's quite likely that you are feeling a sense of longing for something more in life. Perhaps you're also feeling lost, disconnected, or unfulfilled. Maybe you're seeking a sense of purpose, meaning, or direction and thought that this might help you with that.

If that is truly what you seek from this book, I have some news for you – This book will help you find some of the answers, but not all of them.

Let's start with the first one – **You are the source of your problems.** Sorry to have to break it to you so early, but this is how it is.

You may not want to accept it right away, but I'm sure you already have a clue why this is true. And since you've picked this book up, I can also predict that you want to change. Well, if that is the case, you've already taken one step towards it when you started reading.

I've written this book with the purpose of giving you the secret to internal change through the transformative process that we call the spiritual journey. Spiritual journeys are often associated with very clouded judgements. People often confuse them with being tied directly to a specific religion or something similar, when in truth, you might be better off thinking of it as **the science of our being beyond our physical body.**

Few of you might be having these questions in your head right now – *"Beyond the physical body? What's that? Do I need to die in order to experience a spiritual journey?"*

Regarding the details of spiritual journeys, we'll get into it soon. We'll have the rest of the book for it. As for the question of death, I can assure you that you will be very much alive by the time we're done here. After all, you do remember the title of the book, right?

So, let's head right on into our spiritual journey together and find you the better life that you want to live for yourself!

TAKING THE FIRST STEPS

Realizing that the fault lies within us is but the first step in our spiritual journey. To understand more about your journey, there's something that we need to address – our spiritual and true self.

The spiritual or true self is our innermost being, the part of us that is connected to a higher being and to the world around us. It's the metaphysical part of our being that doesn't need to pretend and can exist without worrying about any judgement or fear. It is our existence in the purest form.

In reality, we are yet to find out everything we can about our spiritual self. Different people have different beliefs about it. Some believe that our true self is our eternal and unchanging essence, the part of us that is connected to a higher power or universal consciousness. Others believe that our true self is the part of us that is most closely aligned with our values and purpose in life, and that it can change and evolve over time. Regardless of the truth of the spiritual self, what matters is that it is derived from the same essence of spirituality.

Getting back to the topic of spirituality, it can be difficult to pinpoint where exactly this subject originated because it covers such a broad range of perspectives and much of it still is uncharted territory that is yet to be discovered. From what we do know, however, the roots of it come from the ideas and practices of Hinduism, which many consider to be not a religion but a way of living.

One way to view spirituality is to break it down into layers. At the core of it lies human values that we all seek and expect from the world such as love, compassion, and selflessness. As you move up in those layers, you might find things such as the possibility of a higher power and the yearning for the wisdom of the cosmos. If you're someone who considers themselves aligned with such thoughts, you might be surprised to know that you may have already been in or are currently in a spiritual journey! But no matter where in that journey you may be, even if you're only at the starting line, this book will be your guide moving onwards so that you can make the best of that journey.

Generally speaking, a spiritual journey can be thought of as a process of personal growth and transformation that is guided by one's own spiritual or religious beliefs and values. It can involve seeking out new experiences and insights that help to deepen one's understanding of the self and the world around them, and it can also involve exploring different spiritual practices or traditions. There's also not just one path to spiritual enlightenment –

everyone's path can be different depending on the circumstances that they find themselves in. For some people, having a spiritual master or mentor entails following in their footsteps. Others may take a more independent approach and try to cultivate spirituality through other means and measures.

Again, regardless of the path that one takes, what truly matters is the essence of spirituality and personal development in terms of mental, physical, and spiritual capacity. There are, however, many things that can break us away from our spiritual or true self, leading to a sense of disconnect from our sense of purpose. And now that we have started on our spiritual journey, it is my responsibility to warn you about these deterrents.

STRESS

Stress is one of those things that are necessary in life but can be very harmful in excess. Stress can be a great motivator when we want to push ourselves in life and grow, but without proper moderation, it can have severe consequences on ourselves – on a mental, physical, and spiritual level.

On the physical level, it increases the risk for heart problems, blood pressure, headaches, among other things. On the mental level, we become exhausted, tunnel-visioned, and more self-centered. This eventually leads to feelings of isolation and disconnection from the world around, which in turn, causes us to break away from our spiritual self.

FEAR

Much like stress, fear is another quality we possess that is both necessary and can be harmful to us if left unregulated. It is one of the most powerful emotions that we have and can drive us to take bold steps or cripple us completely and leave us helpless. Being afraid of dying tomorrow, for example, would definitely prompt us to live better today. But it is also this fear that sometimes prevent us from doing what needs to be done. Instead of the fear of death tomorrow, if it's today we're worried about, we might be too afraid to go out of the house, engage with other people, participate in our daily activities, and so on.

In a way, fear controls our survival instinct and makes us desire comfortability when we should be moving forward in life instead. It's not that the desire for comfort is necessarily a bad thing but having it can make us lose our vision and the motivation to grow in life.

There was a moment while I was working a construction job when I had the opportunity to move up. Not too big of a big change in pace but a nice bump in pay and a new title. Instead of pursuing that promotion, however, I let fear in and stop me from putting in my application. At the time, I was financially quite stable, and that comfortability prevented me from taking on the new responsibilities that came with the new position. With that step, or lack thereof, I have probably missed on out many other opportunities down the line. I've made amends with that and understand it wasn't in my path to go that route – but I still think about how I let fear stop me from even trying.

INFLUENCE

Human beings, by nature, are social animals – we care a lot for interpersonal exchanges and are heavily influenced by others around us. We learn from others' experiences and tend to subscribe more naturally to opinions and thoughts that are popular amongst those around us. Every once in a while, however, we are confronted with an opinion or a belief that conflicts with our own.

When that happens, we may find ourselves compromising our values and beliefs in order to fit in or to avoid conflict. Sometimes, it might be a necessity for survival, but regardless of the why, this can lead to a sense of disconnect from our true self. This is especially true when we think that we are morally correct and yet, are unable to express that feeling freely because of external factors.

Like stress, fear, and external influence, there are many other factors as well that may contribute to such disconnects such as anxiety and depression. Starting our journey by recognizing these factors will help us keep ourselves on the right track and maintain a strong connection with our true self. If you're still doubtful about starting this spiritual journey, however, you may be shocked to realize that the chances are quite high that you have already embarked on it through some of your actions. In fact, you picking this book up and reading it is already a step into that journey!

But if you're curious about where a person's spiritual journey starts, let's get into the next section and keep moving on towards building a more fulfilling and spiritually rich life!

SIGNS YOU'RE HEADING TO OR ARE IN A SPIRITUAL JOURNEY

I first learned of the concept of repeating numbers from a friend while working in Oregon and since then, I've considered them a physical sign of a spiritual journey in progress. These numbers each have their own significance for the journey you're currently on.

With repeating numbers, however, I've believed that the meaning behind them can change for each person. While repeating fours meant good to my friend, every time I saw them, something bad happened. I suspect it was due to my mindset at the time, but this was what I noticed. As I have shifted my mindset since then though, I have noticed that repeating numbers can be a sign of good with every sequence having its own meaning. Here is a table to quickly explain numbers and their meanings, based on thelawofattraction.com

111	You're on the right path
222	Pay attention and appreciate the people near you
333	Find balance in your life
444	Remember your roots; call a family member
555	Take the leap! Change is good
666	You're vibrating at a high frequency
777	Take your gut feelings seriously

888	Think realistically and plan for the long term
999	An opportunity to service a lot of people is or will be presented soon

Pay attention if you're noticing numbers pop up lately – the universe is reaching out. They aren't, however, the only signs that you should look out for.

Another sign that you're on a spiritual journey is that you are no longer concerned with what others think of you. Your ego and pride like to play tricks on you and make you think that you need to care about others' opinions of you. The reality is that no one's opinion of you should have an impact on the life you're creating for yourself.

On a similar note, if you're starting to realize that anxiety, panic, and depression creep up on you right when you're wanting to make changes or take leaps, then you're slowly experiencing a partial ego death. **Ego death** happens when you dissolve the selfish prideful ego and rebuild it spiritually. You're experiencing these strong emotions when wanting to make changes because the ego, as I said, is selfish. It wants you to be comfortable and forever in a comfort zone because that's where it flourishes. Right in the space where you think you have the most control, when a spiritual ego does not care for control.

The desire to be of service to others is yet another sign that you're already on a spiritual journey. A big spiritual ideal that grounds us is being of service to others. Wanting to service humankind with your ideas and desires should come to you naturally – it's a sign that you're more aligned with your spiritual self.

One thing that I am experiencing at the moment of writing this is that my body isn't quite able to tolerate things that it used to. Particularly food – I just can't seem to enjoy it like I used to. I'm almost disgusted at the thought of how much of my diet consists of processed food and how incredibly high my sugar intake is. If you're showing signs of not tolerating things you used to since beginning a spiritual journey, then let that be confirmation that you're on the right path.

I recently read a book on chakras and how they're each represented by a color. Apparently, it's good to feed our bodies healthy foods of those colors to feed our souls appropriately. While I wouldn't yet call myself an expert on chakras, I can see how much sense that makes considering how our body reacts to healthy foods in contrast to processed foods.

These are only just a few examples that indicate that you're already on a spiritual journey. And trust me – most of us already are, in some form or other.

Experiencing trauma can also push a person on a spiritual journey as it teaches you how to deal with such intense experiences and their aftermaths in a healthy manner.

TRAUMA RESPONSE WALL BUILDING

We human beings have an incredible superpower that allows us to deal with any kind of trauma or tragic memories by compartmentalizing them and almost forgetting about them in our daily lives. We usually call it building mental walls. But this ability to forget, as it protects us in some cases, also does us harm. When left alone for too long without properly addressing these traumas, they can manifest through our behavior and actions in various ways, ultimately causing issues like anxiety, depression, and other mental health issues.

Taking the time to healthily process such intense memories can allow us to healthily release the feelings and emotions attached to them. This then allows our true self to become more present and our spiritual path to be seen easier. Processing such memories also allows us to better handle such emotional turmoil in the future and not have to drag these feelings into a relationship. The last thing we want to do is put our unprocessed trauma onto the shoulders of the people we love and care for because it can not only bring them unfair suffering but also strain the relationship itself.

Doctor Randi Gunther published a beautiful article in August of 2021 explaining these defensive walls and how they impact our relationships. In that article, she goes on to explain different triggers and actions that your partner may show that are direct indicators of those walls being built up. While her work seems to be addressing cases of couples only, I think the principle still applies to all of our everyday relationships, not just romantic ones.

MASKING

Another result of experiencing traumatic or intense memories that goes hand-in-hand with wall-building is masking. With masking, we tend to develop masked versions of ourselves to accommodate the likes of certain people. An article by Jenna Fletcher, reviewed by Doctor Lori Lawrenz, goes on to elaborate on the idea behind the multiple masks we can wear as a trauma response, for self-esteem issues or even anxiety. These masks can become a coping mechanism that can affect our lifestyles in an unhealthy manner. When we appear or act differently to please others while masking our true self, we are forced live through the lens of the false self we created.

In my case, I had a past relationship that I just couldn't let go of, which turned into emotional baggage that made me wear masks. I let that unprocessed problem wreak absolute havoc on my mental space. For years it seemed to play a role in how my dating went, how I treated other women, and even how I treated myself. I became a terrible version of myself, and it all stemmed from me building up walls, wearing masks, and in general, not processing what was happening to me. Ultimately, I realized that this was only leaving me disconnected from my spiritual self.

TRAUMA NEEDS PROCESSING

You can probably see now that it can be easy to build up walls and mask ourselves from the public once we've gone through traumatic events or troubles in our life. I'm here to tell you, from experience, that any such events or memories need to be processed – healthily, and without our brain trying to pretend it didn't happen. In other words, we need to face our traumas and troubles instead of running or hiding from them or we will continue to be pushed away from our true selves and into a life of constant emotional turmoil.

It almost seems that the more we push away from our true selves, the more conflicted our life can start becoming, and in the grand scheme of things it makes sense. We want the most authentic version of ourselves to be shown to the world but it's also natural to feel fearful and anxious. There's no doubt we all have felt this way at some point in life, and I would argue most of us have gone through some type of traumatic event or trouble.

So, it would be dumb to think that we can just up and do away with these defense mechanisms and let our true selves shine through. It's not always going to be that easy and to be honest, it might not be so ever. The idea here is that we can recognize patterns or responses to what we've been through and begin to mend and/or process them in order to heal our psyche.

Everyone reacts, processes, and recovers from trauma differently. In an article published in 2015, Professor Jeannie DiClementi from Indiana University goes on to detail this idea. She explains that the goal is not to forget the trauma but healthily acknowledge the fact that the event happened without letting it interfere with our daily life.

I'll agree that it can sound easy on paper, but as I said, everyone processes and heals differently. It is ultimately up to you to find what works for you because – well, as hard as it is to say, the truth is that you are the source of your troubles. When you face adversity, it's up to you to find the solutions. No one is going to solve the problems for you. Your support system or group may encourage you and suggest ideas, but they won't be able to dig you out of the hole you're in.

In this day and age, I feel like we, by now, should have normalized the idea that seeking professional help is okay albeit it has been to a great degree. It is one of the best things to do after experiencing traumatic events. While you're still on your own to find the right solutions to your problems, a therapist can guide you through the process of analyzing your emotions and feelings so that you can make better decisions about yourself.

Had I not gone to therapy to process my own troubles, I don't think any of this would have come about – my spiritual journey, my amazing life, and more so this book. Therapy helped me realize something that I refused to acknowledge for so long – that I am the source of my troubles. I am in my own way.

I sat in pity and misery for a long time, thinking things would just work themselves out or that someone would come in and save me. I had to realize that healing comes from the inside. It results from us getting out of our own way and acknowledging that we want or need help.

If you are in the same boat as I once was, I'll ask you to remind yourself that shit happens and that no one's going to just hand you solutions. I wish it were an easy process – something that can be done like a weekend project – but, unfortunately, I've come to realize from experience that it's not. Some people can take years, some just weeks. It all depends on the person and the injury that they're trying to heal. It's not something that should be forced as doing so only makes the process harder. All of it ties to how well you can analyze yourself from a perspective that's not your own.

Healing and processing can be liberating, and once you start with it, you're most likely to already be on a spiritual journey. What matters next is to understand the process and take the right steps to progress on that journey. And this is exactly the purpose that this book was written to serve.

The truth is, for a long time, I couldn't really confront the situations that I found myself in. I was simply lying down and letting life screw me, as most of us do when we don't understand our purpose.

Chances are that if you're reading this, you are where I once was – cloudy-headed and lost. If that is where you are in life, but not where you want to be, this book might be able to help you get beyond that stage.

2
MENTAL HOUSING

Houses aren't built on faulty foundations and there's a good reason why. They are meant to provide us with security and without a strong enough foundation, we know that it will not live up to our expectations. We know, for a fact, that a foundation contributes the most to the overall strength and safety of a house.

This is also exactly how I view the concept of mental space. A sturdy home for processing needs to be built on a solid foundation, and I hate to be the bearer of bad news yet again, but there are many among us who have shitty foundations. Such people struggle with things such as self-reflection and finding answers from within as their perspective is skewed or flawed from the very beginning.

That's not to say that they themselves are screwed and can't build. It's just that they never had the opportunity to build a strong mental foundation due to the circumstances they've grown up or lived in. For such people, their spiritual journey might have some hiccups at first because they may need to reset their thinking and perspectives in order to be closer to their true self, but once they reestablish their foundation, they are guaranteed to be much better as human beings than before.

I've found that dividing this concept of mental space or the 'foundation' into three separate layers makes a lot of sense. These are the three things that matter most when building a strong foundation:

Being Present

The first thing that matters is always being mentally and emotionally present in the moment. Being present in the moment means that you are gathering the right information that you need in order to do what you set out to do. Being mentally and physically present gives you the ability to remain calm in difficult or stressful situations. Being level-headed and realistic also directly improves your decision-making capabilities since you have better information to base them on. It is also a key component for developing quality relationships, good habits, healthy attitude towards the world, and better self-awareness.

Clear Mental Focus

This is your ability to keep your eyes on the journey. Having clear mental focus will ensure that you do not get distracted and can make confident decisions or solve problems without getting unnecessarily influenced by outside opinions or ideas factoring in.

Connection with Your True Self

Your true self is the most important factor in your foundation. Your spiritual or true self guarantees that authentic energy is present, and you are manifesting genuine ideas. That authentic energy will show itself in relationships, interactions, and let people gravitate more towards you. This energy will ensure that you are living a fulfilling and meaningful life, which eventually will translate to more self-confidence and a greater connection to those around you.

When these three are not present, you have a faulty foundation for your home to rest on. This can cause faults in your journey, which by all means is okay as long as we're maintaining and healing as we go. We're not perfect and falling down can be part of the process, but you have to make sure your eyes don't stray away from the true journey at hand. While I do feel being your true self does the heavier lifting of the three, they are still one and the same for a solid foundation. One shouldn't exist without the other two present.

Mental Walls

Let's return to the topic of mental walls that we've covered before for just a moment and understand the importance of a foundation in its context. Say you experienced something tragic or traumatic and this led you to build mental walls to protect yourself without having to face it again or process it. If your foundation isn't quite strong enough, eventually the weight of these walls can cause everything to come crashing down.

Taking care of this foundation is necessary because it is what helps us experience this life in all of its beauty, including the good and not so good. Think of it as your processing center that helps you stay on top of things and make the best of every moment in life, no matter how unexpected things get. Without it at its best, even the littlest things can wreak chaos on our mental space since we have no way of healthily processing it. When a home is built on that solid foundation, we have a space or area for those chaotic experiences to process and exit as they should.

I'm sure you've had someone say to you at some point in life, "If you keep everything bottled up, eventually, it will explode." I often say the same thing, albeit with a slight difference - "If you don't process your negative energy properly, you will die never having lived at all."

Here's to hoping that I can really drive home this point because it's so important, but in case I didn't, let's consider an extension of this example. Let's consider having a guest come over to your mental 'house'. Let's call this guest adversity.

Adversity waltz's right into your home and now you're stuck with this obnoxious guest shitting all over your rugs. The idea of the mental house is that this unpleasant guest has a place to attempt to wreak havoc while you process the fact that your brand-new rugs now have stinky metaphorical shit all over them. I know it all sounds gross and not ideal but think about your mind attempting to process traumas or trouble without a home built on a solid foundation. Probably not a good place to try and process those things, right?

When the trauma has been processed, you can then let it out along with all of the disgusting feelings that it comes bundled with. Of course, trauma doesn't just live in nothingness forever and we do have times in our lives when the stains in our rugs can remind us of its existence. So, then comes cleaning your house.

The beautiful part of overcoming trauma, triggers, and other obstacles in your life is that you learn to face them better – you know that it might still scare or hurt you, but this time you're more prepared to get through it. So, when those stains in your rugs try to come back to the surface, you know where the shampooer is.

3
IDENTITY

You are not defined by your environment, but rather by your experiences. It may take some time to embrace this philosophy, especially if you've grown up surrounded in an unhealthy environment. I was, and for the longest time, I thought that I would grow up to be just as toxic and unhealthy if I did not get out of that environment. I realized later how incredibly wrong I was.

You see, I'm not the biggest fan of the phrase, "fake it till you make it." But I'll also say that it's not entirely ineffective. 'Faking it' requires you to have confidence in yourself, even if it doesn't come naturally. And this delusional confidence is sometimes just what we need to ensure that we are on the right path.

Confidence is crucial for success and can help you overcome difficult situations. You've probably seen stories of people who have overcome adversity to achieve great things, and it's because they believed in themselves and their abilities. Those things don't just happen, they're direct results of people understanding that they are not products of their environment but products of their mind. This thinking and persistence can take you anywhere in life. Your strength lies in the actions you take and the obstacles you've overcome, and while you aren't in control of your past, I'll be damned if you aren't the controller of your future by the end of this book. After all, you do have the power to shape your future – and you most definitely can, with just the right mindset.

Becoming the best version of yourself takes time, but it's a rewarding journey. Your true self is the version of you that's authentic, genuine, and free from societal pressures. It's the version of you that comes out when you're alone and connected well with your inner self. This true self is centered and peaceful, and experiencing life from this perspective is the best way to go about living it.

Ultimately, you are unique and no one else can be you. By embracing your true self, you'll discover your true worth and find true fulfillment in your life.

PONDERING THE SELF

Since we are already on the topic of our identity and what it truly means to be ourselves, let's take the time to think some thoughts together. Start by thinking about your true authentic self.

What are the characteristics and qualities that make you, you?

Now, let's bring a scenario into the picture. Let's say that you are practicing masking whenever you go to work, college, or school – wherever your second home is. You aren't being your true self. You're keeping your real thoughts and feelings to yourself and pretending to be someone you're not.

How does not being your true self in this situation feel?

Probably crappy. It's like you're having to maintain different versions of yourself to keep up with the different people in your life. Now, imagine the exact opposite scenario. You are happy to be yourself wherever you go. You can freely express yourself and can act confidently in your own skin knowing that you aren't going out of your way to pace with other peoples' rhythm.

How does it feel to maneuver your everyday life being your true self?

How much is your self-worth and confidence boosted now that you are authentically yourself?

How do you think your happiness and well-being will be affected once you've taken the weight of your insincere masks off?

I would imagine you are sensing where I'm going with this and can see that being your true self has much more of a positive impact on your mental health and overall lifestyle than hiding yourself and forcing yourself to be someone you're not for the sake of others.

Reflect on these scenarios for a little. Maybe even think of other similar scenarios where you can compare the effects of being and not being true to yourself. Think about how relationships are shaped, business decisions are made, and how everyday life is affected.

How does being yourself affect your relationships?

What do you think will happen to your confidence and happiness having to pretend to be someone else?

These are just a few ways to help establish the importance of being your true self in every aspect of your life. And you have grasped the importance, now would probably be a good time to figure out some ways to implement the changes that are necessary in your life to be able to stay true to yourself.

Think back on those scenarios and take note of every chance that you've had to show your true self rather than a mask that you put on for the convenience of others. Now, start thinking about how you can start bringing your true self to the surface.

Is it about saying 'yes' more? Is it about saying 'no' more? Is it about picking up a skill or a creative outlet to express how you're feeling? Maybe it's actually going to places that speak to your soul that will really help you bring out your true self – like an open mic or an extempore event. Putting yourself around people that enjoy the same things you enjoy is also a great way to see and feel the greatness of being your true self.

Maybe you're not really ready to be around people at the moment because it's natural, but in that case, maybe you'd benefit from being in a different environment. For instance, going to the park late at night when no one is there or hitting an area of town with low amounts of foot traffic might do you wonders.

Remaining your true authentic self leads to greater fulfillment, more happiness, and deeper connections with those around you. So please, for the sake of you, let your true self shine.

> *"We are not human beings having a spiritual experience. We are spiritual beings having a human experience."*
>
> *- Pierre Teilhard de Chardin*

As the world around us continues to become engulfed with technology and marvelous scientific inventions, it's becoming increasingly important to take a step back and appreciate the power of the human spirit. In a world full of endless distractions and endless opportunities, we can easily become overwhelmed and lose sight of the beauty of our own existence. Taking a moment in the day to be still and reflecting on our own strength and capacity for growth can really help us tap into our inner power and truly be grateful for the life we have been gifted. As a consequence, it can also help us become more connected with our true self.

To put it to exercise straight away, I'd like you to take some time, put the book down for a brief moment and reflect a little bit. Remind yourself of some good memories and how great you felt. Remind yourself also about the challenges that you've faced in life and moved on from. Think about the feelings rushing through your body. Let the time flow with you instead of you flowing with it. You'll soon realize that you are gifted in many ways, having lived through these things, and that will help you be more in control of your being and time.

DEATH ANXIETY

The closer you get to your true self, the more you realize how intertwined we are with the universe. Our creation is of cosmic nature. The dust which rose to tingle our nostrils is, in essence, the same dust that gave us life. Once we've completed our journey on Earth, it is again the same dust that we will return to.

My friends have come to me and said that death is scary, but I can't imagine it's as scary as a life spent worrying about it. When your true self is always present, suddenly death isn't a concern. You realize that grasping the beauty of this life and enjoying it while you're here is what matters.

I'm mentioning this because it was something that came up during the beginning of my journey and I feel like it's something that you may experience as well. I agree that the whole idea that our death is closer than we think might be scary, and it's natural that we might get thrown off-course due to its intimidation. But the truth is that living in the moment is more important than living in the past or the future.

If this is something that does come up on your journey, it might take some deep pondering and acceptance. Professional help might also come in quite handy. Rest assured though – everyone feels a bit death anxious now and then, but with practice, you'll learn to deal with it healthily.

FORGET EVERYTHING ELSE

To wrap this chapter up, here's something that no one will tell you. There are times in life when you'll need to forget about anything else besides yourself. Forget the environment. Forget about poverty. Forget about world peace.

Unless you are in a position that requires you to actively think about these things, you may want to avoid thinking too much about things that are out of your control. I'm not saying that you should completely ignore these things but do so after you become one with your true self.

You are not your situation, and your life is, ultimately, the most important thing for you. Understand that you are amazing. You are worth it. You are the reason I've compiled my journey in this book, and whether you're reading this for the first time or are revisiting it, know that I'll always be thankful to you for going through it with me.

I believe in you.

4
TO SQUARE ONE

Before we get back to the serious stuff again, allow me to indulge you in a story that will be in the book following this one. The story of how and where I began my journey. The story of how my life, in more ways than one, turned upside down.

The year was 2008. Skinny jeans were newly popular, heavy music was at a pivotal point and I still went to church.

I've been curious my whole life, and so, naturally, attending church was an experience. I had to question everything. My curious nature begged my brain to acquire as much knowledge on everything crossing my path. And so, I asked questions. Lots of questions.

It got to the point where I was being mocked for it. It didn't help that I didn't care to try to fit in or put in the effort for friendships. I moved around a ton as a kid, and so establishing solid friendships was far from my priority.

The mocking would soon turn into giggles and whispers, which was followed by some name calling. At twelve years old, I started to learn just how real emotions were. How real it was to be sad. It was quite a few years later that I realized that the church wasn't the source of my depression and there might be a deeper reason for it. These kids that were around me at the time had no true understanding of empathy. It was something that I excelled in though.

I wasn't born into the best of situations, so having to grow up faster than I should have kind of forced me to perceive life through a different lens. These kids had no real worries, and while I guess I didn't either, having been on the receiving end of their negative energy, I learned the true meaning of empathy and understanding.

At first, I used to not give much thought to their bullying, but carried out over time, it can begin to change your mental space. So, I acted to the degree I thought was appropriate given my age. I shut down. I kept it cool around my mom because I didn't want to bring any attention to the situation at church. She had enough to worry about anyway. Looking back, I realize I should've said something – but I didn't.

So, my sadness began. I stopped trying to talk so much and shut myself in. I built a lot of those walls that we talked about. The one constant in my life at the time was now becoming the one thing I wanted no part of, and I slowly started to feed myself to the darker side. Ultimately, I grew to hate the very thing that gave me hope for the future.

6 years later...

A warm spring day lit my window as I woke up, still tired from the night before. I checked my phone habitually and hopped out of bed, not realizing today's the day. I got ready and made some phone calls. I started the day with some cereal and then headed over to my dad's house.

My parents lived on opposite ends of town, which I didn't mind because the half an hour drive was really enjoyable and a good time for me to be with my own thoughts for a little while. Nothing about this day was off yet. In fact, everything about this day was lining up to be great.

It was Senior Ditch Day, and the plan was to head to the river after I took my dad's truck and picked my friends up. It took a little convincing, but I managed to get the keys from him. We weren't planning too much – maybe a couple drinks with some other friends and then on our way to do some other ditch day activities.

We reached the river and were only getting settled in when one of my friends persuaded me to take the truck into the little hills that ran along the river. I obliged. Down a hill, up a hill, and then finally to the top of a plateau we went. Now, I just needed to park the truck and we could get to the fun stuff. Being in the jolly mood that I was in, I had a thought – let's do a quick donut to get sone dirt flying. But then, things happened and before I could react, the truck started to head in another direction. I looked at my passenger and saw the ground coming at us at full speed. I did my best to grab him and pull up before we made impact but as the sound of crunching metal and shattering glass hit my eardrums, everything went black.

I opened my eyes to a very different scene. I was watching my body, from above. I could see everything happening on the ground in that present moment. A tipped over truck, a seemingly lifeless body of mine, and people who were starting to take notice.

In the moments of this in-and-out of bird's eye view and blackness, I was sent to what I would later find out is near death. From what I remember, I was standing alone in a field of grass. It wasn't just grass though – something was different about it. It was just perfect. The way it flowed in the wind was like its whole purpose was made exactly for my feet to walk on.

Before I could start registering anything else, I was suddenly embraced by a warmth I had never felt before. All at once, I was feeling love, peace, and comfort light years beyond what I thought was even possible. This warmth covered me and guided me through this other realm. As I walked, it seemed like every question I could have had been answered before I could ask it. Around me were beautiful trees, far off mountains, and everything seemed to be living as one. As I breathed, the world around me seemed to breathe with me – all of us in constant oneness, together.

As the realization hit that I might very well be on the path away from this world, my sight was guided to the sky where I saw two versions of myself arguing. One of them was the perfect professional – clean cut and dressed as if I could walk into a job interview. The other looked like he had just been in a bar fight and was ready for another. They continued to argue as I started passing out again and was brought back to a bird's eye view of myself. Then I began going in and out of what I can only assume is consciousness. The episodes finally subsided after a while and I managed to become conscious for good, waking up to stare at the underside of the truck.

I managed to get up and walk a bit – until I noticed that everything was happening in slow motion. I presume this was due to the shock of everything catching up with my consciousness. I moved to the other side of the truck and went inside to grab some things I left behind, like my phone and gym bag.

Unbeknownst to me, a few others had piled into the bed of the truck, and as I went to grab my things, I looked to my left to see something I will not wish upon my greatest enemy if I ever have one.

One of the guys was crushed under the weight of the truck.

As you might expect, I went into shock once again. I grabbed my things and headed towards the river where most of us were still. In and out of my shock, I was trying to piece together exactly what was going on. As people ran by me, screaming, towards the truck, I became overwhelmed with a sense of calmness and nobody around me was making a sound.

The world around me became so quiet that I could hear the water running and gliding over the rocks.

As I kept walking, a young lady pulled me to the side and started wrapping my arm with a shirt. Apparently, in the midst of everything, I didn't even realize I was being drained as blood was gushing out of my arm. To this day I have no idea how my arm was cut up so deeply.

As she wrapped my arm, my phone began vibrating. I looked at it in disbelief.

Mom…

I answered, afraid of the conversation about to unfold.

"Hi bub, how's your day going?" My mother said cheerily.

Nothing came out of my mouth for about a solid 5 seconds. "Mom.," I said as I regained composure, "I was in an accident, and I think someone is dead."

I was almost shaking at this point. The commotion of the rush slowly started coming to me as I explained the location to my mom, hung up, and then began dialing 911. The rest of the day ensued, I was eventually taken away in an ambulance and treated for my injuries at the local hospital.

What took place over the next couple months was nothing short of profound. It was the one thing that changed my entire life.

I spent the rest of the spring break in my room, only leaving to use the restroom. I was visited by friends and family, but the images and thoughts of that day remained vividly replaying in my mind. Nothing seemed to help me process what was going on.

I received death threats; social media had field days with my name and going back to school seemed impossible. I was also removed from my dad's insurance at the request of the insurance company and told to go to therapy at the request of my parents.

I now know how helpful therapy can be. but at that time, I was too ignorant to know just how good it is for you when you truly need it. It took me a couple of sessions to be diagnosed with what is called an NDE. A Near Death Experience is, as the name itself suggests, when someone is brought close to death, often with such experiences or sensations as the ones I described earlier.

This was a hard concept to grasp given the circumstances. You could imagine I was experiencing, and still do to some extent, survivor's guilt pretty harshly. Sleeping was near non-existent as I stayed awake night after night, trying to process these things over and over. Therapy helped sort out the huge mess in my head, but I felt as if there were many questions that I needed to find answers to on my own.

I like to think that it was at this point that my spiritual journey began. I believe everything does happen for a reason and is a part of our journey here, but I didn't necessarily want to die to realize I was going to begin this path.

As months passed, I would eventually graduate and begin working. My life would then continue to be a constant learning and growing process where I would explore my mind like never before, eventually landing me in front of this keyboard.

The truth is – shit does happen. It's how we clean up the shit that matters the most. I was faced with several forks in the road after the accident I was in. I could let this situation wreak havoc in my head without hope for answers, and end up like the people in my environment I swore to not be like. Or I could get up and clean this shit up.

And so, I began cleaning.

As I mentioned, I spent time picking apart my mind for answers, reading books, going to therapy, and studying. I spent all this time looking for an answer before realizing that I am the answer.

All I needed to do was simply 'want' to get better. The act of me wanting to find acceptance led me toward acceptance. I'm not saying you can go through traumatic events and just want acceptance.

Everyone deals with these things differently and it's just how mine eventually came to me.

I learned that you have to want to better yourself because life won't hand you what you're looking for sometimes. It's up to us to objectively look at the situation and ask ourselves questions. More importantly, it's up to us to dig deep enough to get the answers we're looking for. Our minds are powerful beyond measure. We simply need to use it.

I do have a long journey ahead of me but I'm confident I have reached a point where I can share my experience and use the knowledge I gained to help people, maybe like yourself, start healing and finding their answers.

You deserve to heal.

You deserve to see life.

The world deserves you.

You deserve You.

5
WHAT'S PRACTICE WITHOUT EQUIPMENT?

What kind of teacher would I be without providing some tools to add to your belt?

This is where I would recommend a highlighter, notepad, or maybe even just take some pictures. I'm going to list and describe the things I use to maintain this true-self experience and the ways I assist myself in making it easier.

I wish I could offer a one size fits all piece that everyone could make use of, but the truth is what works for me might not always be what works for you. The beauty of it though is that once you find your process, it's like opening the door to a new world. Hopefully, you'll find your way to the door from hints of my knowledge and experience. The key to opening, however, is completely going to be your own journey ahead.

I will preface this whole list by saying that the best way to get started in finding your true self is self-evaluation and consistent questioning. Not over questioning just for the sake of it but yearning for knowledge beyond where you think your mind has limits. Self-evaluation looks something like:

"Who am I?"

"What is my purpose?"

"What makes me, me?"

"What is it that truly matters to me the most?"

And so on.

These questions tend to start turning the gears in your mind and help with sorting out the mess that may be in there. For those who are in the midst of their spiritual journey, these questions can help with reassurance and the confirmation of one's connection with one's true self. If you ever revisit this book after you've gotten better at staying true to yourself, I'm sure you'll see what I mean when you ask yourself these same questions again.

As I've said before, our true self is calm and peaceful. The true self is allowed to simply be. This allows us to enjoy and experience our life as it should be.

Which leads to the first practice and arguably the most popular one.

MEDITATION

Meditation, originating as far back as 1500 BCE, is the practice of diving into our own mind, centering ourselves, and pondering deeply. Mostly associated with Buddhism and Hinduism, meditation is practiced among many walks of life and faith.

To meditate, I recommend finding a quiet place that you are comfortable being in, sit down, and start relaxing your breath. In through the nose and out through the mouth, usually to the count of four. Every breath in you is becoming more relaxed, every breath out you are exhaling your worries and troubles. You are going to notice your mind wandering – let it, but only enough so that you can still remain centered and focused on what you're meditating for.

As you wander though, start taking mental notes as to what is taking place. The idea of meditation is to remain in the present moment and let our thoughts flow instead of letting them run at each other chaotically.

You should always close your meditation sessions with kindness. When you're ready, you are going to slowly open your eyes, stay relaxed for a second and take your environment back in.

Recognize your thoughts, emotions, and the way you maneuvered this session. It's okay to be a little lost before your first meditation session. If you need easy tutorials to get started, I always suggest going to YouTube and listening to some guided meditation videos. That is a good way to get started with the basics and figure out what style of meditation works best for you.

I've tried a ton of meditation methods and, realistically, at the end of the day, whatever works for you, run with it. I have meditated in my car, sitting down, standing up, in a pool, and every scenario was beautiful in its own way. So, really, don't be afraid to try whatever comes to your mind.

READING

Reading can also have amazing benefits towards a spiritual journey. Learning from people who have already been through things or are masters at their craft is a sure-fire way to gain both theoretical and practical knowledge. It's also a great way to see other perspectives and see where yours can align or contrast.

Reading is arguably the best way to gain an understanding of your own spirituality and challenge your beliefs, which ultimately leads to outstanding personal growth. I can attest to the fact that reading was the most beneficial thing for me when beginning my journey because it gave me outside opinions, spiritual stories for me to analyze, and wisdom that's been passed down for many years.

Think about it – *what is there to lose trying out a new book?*

A fun pass time, whether you're still on the fence or enjoy books in general, is to go down to a bookstore and spend some time in your favorite section. Pick some books to skim through and see if anything sticks out. Then read, and read, and read.

Challenging yourself to read is a great way to keep yourself interested and motivated. You can set a short-term goal such as reading at least 10 pages a day and then a long-term goal such as reading an X number of books per year. Doing so can also help you maintain a reading schedule and get a sense of achievement when you reach these goals.

MINDFUL WALKING

Mindful walking is one of those amazing tools that no one talks about. It can solidly your mindfulness tremendously and help you revaluate your life and self while keeping your body active.

The idea here is to walk and become very aware of the present and, more so, aware of yourself.

When I walk, I like to consistently make sure I am in tune with myself and meditatively breathing. I also like to express gratitude towards whatever comes to my mind. I will express thanks to Mother Earth and the beauty that I get to experience everyday – sometimes something as simple as grass. I will send good energy to the people in my life and express gratitude to their part in my human experience, and then I will reflect on myself and embrace the path I have paved so far. I also make sure to let go of any judgements or expectations as I walk. This helps develop greater focus and increase my awareness of the present. It's also good to have a question or multiple questions ready prior to your walk. This can help guide the walk in a better direction, especially if you're just starting out.

I look at mindful walking as a way to recenter myself when I'm not in the space to have a meditation session or after having lunch at work.

CLEANING

Now, this might be a bit controversial for some, but I find cleaning very rejuvenating. Physically and mentally.

I am sure we have all been in a situation – there's a pile of laundry, a sink full of dishes, and a room to clean, but you just can't bring yourself to do it. Then, you finally motivate yourself and get to cleaning your room, doing laundry, or finally running that errand you've been putting off. And then, when it's all done, there's a deep sense of satisfaction and achievement. I can attest that it is a situation I find myself in quite often. And I have found that cleaning the space around you can directly relate to your mental space.

Room is a mess = head is a mess.

This may not be true for everybody, but for me personally, if my room is a mess, rest assured my attitude and self are all out of whack.

So, how can you use this to your advantage? Well, it's simple, clean. Set a day of the week when you know that you can get up, handle business, and stick to it. I've found that if I can handle my cleaning days on my days off then my head space during the week is better because I'm not so cluttered by the physical space around me.

This turnaround of cleanliness works just as well the other way around. Sometimes, we just need to sit back and clean our head space. Meditation, self-care, gratitude sessions – whatever it is that you can utilize to clean up your mental space, use it. Doing so can bring you in the right space to finally work out the motivation to get to the 'physical' cleaning.

It's really amazing how the simplest things are almost like life cheat codes.

JOURNALING

To be straight with you, I barely find myself journalling. But I do know that it's incredibly effective at some things. Ironically, journalling is also something I recommend to others very often, even though it's not my personal go-to activity. It's easy to get started and doesn't take time – which is perfect for people who are busy and just want to get started with their spiritual journey.

It's not that I have never used it in my life though. The few times I've used it to maneuver various situations in my life, it worked amazingly. For example, I came across a couple business decisions I needed to make and instead of pondering them, I just started journaling my thoughts on them. Eventually, this landed me directly into my confident final answer. The act of me simply jotting down my ideas forced my brain to declutter and think a little more clearly than it otherwise would have.

You might be surprised to know at this point that it was my mom who introduced me to journalling. She describes it as a way to declutter what's going on upstairs, and I can see how. It is literally the easiest way to give form to your mental clutter so that you have an easier time arranging it in your head.

Decluttering by means of journaling is also a form of cleaning! So, you're technically using two tools at once. It is also an excellent way to track your life as you experience it. When I journal it's usually to look back on my progress towards my goals. I've found that it can be a confidence boost to look back and see how far you've come from the beginning of a journey to the present. Moreover, journaling is also a great activity after or during some mindful walking.

So, go pick up a journal if you haven't already!

YOGA

With us already on the subject of me preaching what I don't practice, let's look into another amazing process that I hardly find myself engaging in – yoga. My reasons for it are quite simple – I find it difficult to fit into my schedule, and as such, I've found that it's not my cup of tea yet. Maybe sometime in the future.

Yoga today may be different from what it was thousands of years ago, having originated from Hinduism much like the concept of meditation, but the principles are mostly still the same. It is a great way to explore your mind, body, and spirit. It also can teach you great life skills like balance, humility, and perseverance. Plus, it also keeps you in good shape. Yoga's true potential, however, as a means to increase one's spiritual freedom is much more than just this. It's not surprising to learn that people have dedicated their whole lives to try and figure out the secrets of the body, the mind, and the spirit, using yoga as a means to do it.

Head on down to your local yoga studio or even find a gym that does yoga sessions and sign up! You never know how much you will actually enjoy it, and if you don't, then you know you're one step closer to finding what works for you.

DETACHMENT

Now getting back to the steps that I actually use in my life; detachment is again one of those that aren't really popular or talked about. The concept of it might be a bit hard for most people at first, but the general idea is that you let go of any and all expectations and ideas of outcomes.

I say this will be hard for most because we tend to establish ideas for situations immediately after thinking about the situation itself. Instead, what we need to do is just experience the situation as is. Putting an expectation on something or setting an idea for an outcome means you've already lost because you have given yourself a false sense of reality and comfort.

Practicing detachment can be especially difficult if you're an anxious person like I am, but it will undoubtedly get easier and easier with time and patience. This, in turn, can also help you learn how to control your anxious mind.

The idea of letting go of any outcomes or expectations means you will be letting go of your predetermined ideas of how things in your life or current situation play out. That means letting go of your desire to control situations. You will have to learn to surrender and let go instead of wanting to control. When you practice detachment, you will want to remind yourself that the outcome doesn't matter, because you're remaining in the present moment rather than the future.

We all know how important it is to be able to live in the present, but I'll let ancient China's one of the most prominent philosophers reiterate this:

> *"If you are depressed you are living in the past.*
>
> *If you are anxious you are living in the future.*
>
> *If you are at peace you are living in the present."*
>
> **- Lao Tzu**

Let this quote remind you that it's okay to not be okay. Understand that sometimes you need to lose control of everything around you to gain more control of yourself. Most of our internal issues are usually products of our attachment to our past or future.

We also like to be very attached to our jobs, relationships, and even money. We can even develop attachments to the labels put on us since birth. These labels may be based on facts, but they are most inconsequential. They are, after all, labels; they are not you. You may have labels such as 'brother', 'sister', 'lazy', 'too active', and so on – but if any of those things change, you don't stop being you.

The easiest beginning to detachment is distinguishing between reality and your ego. Your ego lays out expectations in your mind. For instance, you may think that if I don't get a new car by this certain time in my life then I'm a failure, or if I'm not in this particular point in my career by a certain age then I failed.

The truth is, regardless of the outcome, you are still you and getting those things you want can still come. But continuously asking "when?" is only giving you a sense of false reality. Separating the ego and reality allows you to objectively think about yourself and the situations you're in. Once you're able to do that, you start being more present and be in control of your reality.

Once you have learned to detach from the outcome, you start opening up the endless possibilities that can happen.

CLEARING ENERGY

Moving on to the next one, learning to get rid of the extra energy in you can be a great way to keep your mental space clear. This is enormously helpful in creating a beautiful spiritual path, and if not done, can be detrimental to your spiritual journey.

Over and over, we waste our time doing things that give no progression to our purpose. Take a look around you and start paying attention to everything you're putting your energy into. Whether it be social media, relationships, or really anything you can take note of that is taking up or feeding off your energy.

Now, for the lack of a better visual, imagine your spiritual energy like a physical and big beam of energy shooting out of your chest. That beam represents your purpose and drive. Now, start adding other beams to represent everything in your life taking up your energy. As you add more things your main beam starts becoming smaller and smaller, to account for the other things in your life, thus taking energy from your purpose and drive energy. Take this into consideration when you start accounting for everything in your life taking up your energy.

The idea here is to eliminate or lessen everything not worthy of taking that energy away from your purpose and drive, and instead feed that excess energy into your purpose and drive. The more we can remove and put back into our purpose beam, the more fulfilled we tend to be.

Write some things that may be taking away from your purpose or time.

GIVING

Sort of falling under the discussion of 'karma', but also geared toward the enrichment of society as a whole, the practice of giving can do wonders for your life. Here's what I do personally. I will take a gift with me everywhere I go. This gift can be anything from a compliment, a smile, or even an actual physical gift. The idea here is to receive with thanks and give without keeping tabs. You want to keep the wealth of kindness in constant rotation, creating a more peaceful and loving experience around you.

Try to make giving a daily practice. Everywhere you go, bring a gift – even if it just your presence and a smile as sometimes the effect of even the simplest gifts can go much further than you realize.

KARMA

Karma, both good and not good, is a wonderful experience. You have probably heard that saying "What goes around comes around." Well, that is karma in its essence.

Many people tend to assume karma to be a negative consequence when in reality karma is both the negative and positive experience after our actions.

One of my favorite producers, !llmind, has a terrific way of explaining karma. Imagine you are holding a rubber band, the rubber band will represent karma, and your hands will represent your actions. Your hands, or actions so to speak, will stretch that rubber band further and further out.

Eventually that rubber band is going to come back and give you that same energy that you were putting into it, whether that is good or not good. That is essentially karma. The idea here is to feed good energy into your rubber band so when it comes back, you are hit with good energy.

Actions are also nothing without the intention behind them. Someone doing good things but not with good intentions is still going to receive bad karma because of their intention. Your intention behind your actions will say a lot more than the action itself in the long run. So, when you are feeding good actions into your rubber band be sure your intentions are at the same level.

EXPRESSING GRATITUDE

I can say this now with a certain degree of certainty – the journey that you're embarking on right now will come with defeat, victory, turmoil, happiness, sadness, as well as many other events and emotions. As such, it can be quite easy to get tunnel visioned on the things that matter less. Keeping sight of what is important and what truly matters might become a challenge, but we know that it's necessary. And so, sometimes, we need to take steps to ensure that we don't lose sight of that so that we don't find ourselves derailed from the journey.

Here's where expressing gratitude by looking back at the things that supported you and helped you grow comes in excellent purpose. I personally have gratitude sessions every morning while enjoying some tea and breakfast. These sessions don't always have to be about your past and there are no hard and bound rules. You could be thankful to the weather, the wind, the cup of coffee in your hand, or that random stranger that helped you out in a time of crisis – everything goes. All that matters is that your gratitude comes from the heart.

The idea behind doing so is to express thankfulness for things you might otherwise not acknowledge, or things you might have overlooked, such as the warmth of the sun, or a phone call from a family member. Your expression of thanks feeds the universe the acknowledgement of your willingness to not forget the little things. In simpler terms, you're showing the universe you care and are thankful for everything, even if life isn't going how you are wanting at the moment.

Take some time every day, in the midst of your daily groove, to express thanks. Even if it is for something as simple as grass.

NATURE

I had to save the best one, in my opinion, for last. Nature. The easiest way to experience something bigger than yourself is to spend some quality time in the company of mother nature. It allows us to disconnect from our fast-paced, technology-filled lives and reconnect with a larger part of the universe around us. Plus, you also have an opportunity for physical activity, which can help release endorphins to boost mood and improve your overall health.

Make a trip to a local park, visit a national forest, and try everything in between – I'm serious. Nature is such a vibrant way to reconnect, recenter, and reestablish your true self that I look at it as the grand slam of my spiritual journey. The fresh air, mental cleaning, mindful walking, and time that is spent with yourself or people you love - it hits so many nails on the head. It is my go-to for anyone that asks me where to start or maintain their spiritual journey. A few of them have even told me that doing so helped them find a new perspective on life and a sense of awe and wonder at the beauty and complexity of the natural world.

Nature can also be a source of inspiration, helping to tap into creativity and imagination. It's not hard to imagine why so many artists and creative people prefer the company of nature every once in a while. Whether it's a quiet walk in the woods, or a day spent exploring a national park, spending time in nature can help to nurture the mind, body, and spirit.

So, here were the ideas that I promised you at the beginning of the chapter. All of these practices and ideas work wonders on keeping your spiritual journey thriving. Some of them might be a bit difficult and some of them easy to follow, but maintaining any of them will ensure that you've taken one step towards always being your true self and paving a good spiritual path for yourself.

I take time to incorporate many of these into my daily life – to the point where my day doesn't feel complete if I haven't done at least some of them. I always recommend finding ways to include these practices in your daily life, so they almost become habitual and won't give you feel like you're doing a task or chore.

The idea behind all of these is to strengthen your routine with the practices previously mentioned while also strengthening your mental foundation. In spiritual language, allowing your foundation to be built properly and your mental house to flourish.

6
YOUR TOOLS IN ACTION

Now that you have the tools that I've shared with you, it's time to put them to use. In this chapter, my goal is to get you to start implementing at least a few of them in your life so that you can progress on your spiritual journey.

MEDITATION

Meditation can be difficult to start in the sense that it takes patience, and some people might find it boring. When I am introducing someone to the idea, I always suggest starting with small doses at first. So, perhaps, when just starting out, do a 5-minute meditation in the morning before work and then another 5 minutes when you get home. Then, as you become adjusted and comfortable, raise that to 10 minutes, twice a day. The sweet spot, where most people will recommend, is 15 minutes, twice a day, once in the morning and once in the evening. Once you start doing meditation sessions, it gets easier and more fun.

But as I have mentioned previously, meditation in simple terms is quiet mind pondering. So, if you want to meditate in a swimming pool while floating on your back, please do so. Some might not agree with me, but this is what I strongly believe. For me, it's about being in your comfort zone and accomplishing intense mindfulness.

Here is a simple meditation routine for you to try if you're looking for something right now:

1. Sit in a cross-legged position, ensuring that you're sitting upright.
2. Begin to focus on your breaths (I like the four breaths in, four breaths out method).
3. Inhale through the nostrils, becoming more relaxed, and exhale through the mouth, letting your worries and troubles go.
4. As you become more relaxed, scan your body and take notice of any sensations in your body.
5. As your mind starts to wander, keep focusing on your breathing.

6. Let your mind wander and take mental notes of what your mind is telling you.

7. When you're ready, begin to open your eyes and remain relaxed before ending your session with kindness.

I wish you peace, love, and happiness on your spiritual journey. If you need any more guides or details on meditation strategies, feel free to reach out to me on my social media which can be found on my about me page. Remember that meditation is a personal practice, and it's about finding what works best for you. Keep exploring and practicing, and may you find the inner peace and balance you seek.

MINDFUL WALKING

Mindful walking is simple - just walk with intention. Not every walking session will result in a big problem-solving epiphany, but you should aim to ponder and accomplish something, even if it's as small as deciding to eat better that day or how to approach a new project.

Start by simply walking and taking in your environment, then focus on your breath. Find a rhythm and walk to it, whether it's a calm and peaceful rhythm or something else. Next, begin expressing gratitude, pondering questions, dissecting your diet, or whatever you planned to think about prior to the walk.

If you just want to walk mindfully to recenter and get some steps in, that's okay too. Here's a bonus tip: if you know that you're easily distracted by your phone, leave it at home or in your pocket during your walk.

CLEANING

Like I said earlier, this one is big for me. When my space is messed up, I'm messed up. My cleaning schedule goes as such:

Big clean on Sunday. I'm talking scrubbing, mopping, vacuuming, taking out the trash, the whole ordeal. I choose a weekend day to accomplish this because it sets up my weekdays, when I'm usually the busiest, for success. During the week, I can happily do small tasks like washing the dishes from dinner, cleaning my work area and little clean ups around the bathroom or closet. The same can go for your mental cleaning. I leave that up to just how I'm feeling that day so that's what I usually suggest but you can easily mirror the physical schedule to the mental if that's what might work best for you.

READING

I aim to read two books per month, for a total of 24 books per year. I prefer to set an annual goal rather than pace myself monthly, as some months I might devour several books while others I may only manage to squeeze in one.

Of course, your reading pace is entirely up to you. If you're new to reading regularly, I suggest starting with 10-15 pages a day so you can ease into the habit and see how you like it. For more experienced readers, read as much or as little as you want - read 100 books a year if that's what you enjoy!

Create a goal,

Find your pace,

Adjust goal, if necessary,

Read on!

JOURNALING

Consider getting a journal! I cannot stress enough how much this simple tool can change your life.

Whether you use it for doodling, problem-solving, or even writing a book, a journal can become your best friend and help you organize even the toughest mental messes. (Yes, I wrote down the ideas, points, and even some chapters for this book in a small $2 journal from Target.)

Your journaling method is entirely up to you. Some people prefer a daily log-style, while others opt for a weekly update. Personally, I have journals lying around for whatever random reason I feel like writing down. I have journals with poems, song lyrics, and even terrible drawings I thought were amazing when I was 17.

However, my favorite kind of journal is a personal one. These are the ones where I can use my pen to write down my thoughts and feelings and figure out solutions or even just vent.

Your journal can be whatever you want it to be.

YOGA

Yoga not only has incredible health benefits but also amazing mental health benefits. For many years, yoga has been a fundamental physical activity of spirituality and a way to train our bodies and minds to become more self-aware and observant. If you're not familiar with any poses or techniques, I recommend getting to a studio as soon as possible. Alternatively, if you're a DIY kind of person, a yoga mat and YouTube can also go a long way.

DETACHMENT

It is time to recognize your attachment and the emotions that come with it. When we become attached to a certain outcome or expectation, we immediately set ourselves up for failure. By doing so, we put a premature finish to something that may just be starting, and when things don't go as we planned, we tend to blame external factors rather than the actual problem which is within us. Perhaps, it is because we find comfort in what we already know, instead of embracing the unknown.

Detachment, on the other hand, involves recognizing our patterns of setting expectations and taking action to rid ourselves of them. You could start by journaling every time you put an expectation on something or, alternatively, by meditating and telling your subconscious to stop seeking comfort in the known. It might sound a little straightforward, but it is important to keep in mind that we tend to love the known and what gives us comfort, which is why we naturally gravitate towards it.

Recognize your patterns, investigate them, formulate a plan, and execute it to aid in the extinction of these patterns. It all starts with recognizing that you are setting expectations and not embracing the unknown.

CLEARING ENERGY

The process of clearing energy can be different for each person, but for me, I tried to make it as easy as possible. I would get a piece of paper and write down everything that was taking up my energy. This included the gym, work, side hustles, family time, and running errands. It's important to account for everything that's taking up your energy. Then, I separated everything into two categories: things that were necessary and things that I could part with. I even took work and found ways to feed my purpose during breaks or when it was slow.

In practice, clearing energy is simply cutting off the activities, people, and anything else that takes away from our purpose or passions. It can seem a little selfish, but the intention behind it is good. You're not cutting off all these things menacingly or even at all in some cases. For some things, I slowly weaned myself off, like wasting my lunch breaks talking to my coworkers. The hardest part for me was cutting people off, some just a little to make space and others completely for the sake of my life goals. Remember, your circle is a reflection of what you'll achieve. If you're surrounded by negative people, you'll probably end up being negative as well. If you're surrounded by encouraging and uplifting people, you'll have a much better time trying to maintain positivity in your life.

It's all about dissecting your daily routine and finding what isn't feeding your purpose. Energy plays a huge role in your life, so use it wisely.

GIVING

Let's talk about giving. It's something that can enrich both the giver and the receiver, and it doesn't have to be a big gesture. Giving can come in many forms, from a simple smile or compliment to a physical gift, knowledge, or help. The goal of giving is to further enrich society with love and positivity.

You can incorporate giving into your daily life in small ways, such as complimenting someone on their clothing or bringing a bottle of wine or a dish to a dinner party. Remember that giving has no limits. As Elizabeth Bibesco said,

> *"Blessed are those that can give without remembering and receive without forgetting."*

KARMA

I'll make this one quick:

Good actions, good intentions produces good karma.

Good actions, not good intentions produces not good karma.

Not good actions, not good intentions produces not good karma.

Not good actions, good intentions produces not good karma.

Your actions and intentions must both reflect your true self to acquire good karma. It all starts with the thought behind the action.

EXPRESSING GRATITUDE

Gratitude, in its simplest form, is giving thanks. Being thankful for what you have and have accomplished instead of thinking of what you don't have or haven't accomplished. I, personally, include gratitude sessions here and there in my meditation sessions or sometimes while just having my morning tea.

I also suggest it to everyone I talk to – to incorporate gratitude in their life more, especially if they're not feeling one hundred percent all the time. It is easy – whatever you're thankful for, simply express your feeling for what it is instead of worrying about what isn't. Appreciate what's with you in the present moment and what you have previously accomplished rather than what might lie ahead in life. Take a moment every day to say thanks for something small and then once a while, include a family member or a friend as well!

I'll go as far to say that whenever you are feeling doubts or not worthy of something, look back on your past achievements and accomplishments be thankful for those – it can really help you boost your morale. Gratitude can be confirmation that you've progressed, just as long as you don't let it flood your ego with praises.

NATURE

I believe most of us can easily access nature, even if it's just a nearby park with more trees than the others. Incorporating nature into your spiritual journey is simpler than you might think.

Personally, I set aside certain days weeks in advance for a simple hike. During each hike, my goal is to stay off my phone completely, except for music during the climb, and fully appreciate what Mother Earth has to offer.

For those in school, I recommend finding a local park to study and meditate in once a week. Regardless of your schedule, aim to spend as much time as possible in nature. Try changing your location each time until you have a playlist of scenic spots to visit.

7
FAILING IS NECESSARY

Undertaking a spiritual journey is not a task for the faint of heart. It's the chapter in this book that I fear may cause some people to lose interest and give up before they even begin. The initial stages of a spiritual journey can be uncomfortable and frightening, and for a long time, I tended to play it safe, avoiding big risks.

I was the type of person who participated in fun activities simply for the experience, without pushing myself to my limits. Looking back, there are moments from my earlier years that I wish I could redo, but then I wouldn't be where I am today - typing away on this screen and sharing with you the idea that our past choices do not have to determine our future ones. We are the product of our thoughts, and we should never forget that.

This chapter is the most difficult one for me to write because I have to admit that failure is inevitable on this journey. It's the cruelest part of the human experience, but it also makes the rewards that much more satisfying. There will be two types of people who read this book - those who finish and take action, and those who set the book aside for years before realizing they should have taken the leap. I hope you are the former and take these words to heart.

FAILURES ARE STEPPING STONES

Failure is an inevitable part of the human experience, and it is often seen as something to be avoided or minimized. In the realm of spirituality, failure can actually play a crucial role in helping you learn to embrace things from an open-minded perspective. By embracing failure and learning from it, we can grow and evolve on our spiritual journeys, and ultimately find greater fulfillment and success.

Failures in life often provide opportunities for self-reflection and introspection. When we fail, we try to confront our own limitations and weaknesses, and this can be a valuable opportunity to gain a deeper understanding of ourselves. Through self-reflection, we can identify areas for improvement and growth, and develop a greater sense of self-awareness.

Failure can sometimes also serve as a catalyst for change and transformation. When we fail, we may feel motivated to make changes in our lives in order to avoid similar failures in the future. This can include changing our beliefs, behaviors, or habits, and can ultimately lead to personal growth and evolution.

I'm sure you've failed quite a few times in life – after all, no one is perfect. And I'm also sure that you've learned things from at least some of them. These lessons could have ranged from practical strategies for overcoming obstacles, to a deeper understanding of the human condition and the nature of reality – and I'm sure they've helped you further down the line. This is how you learn everything in life – from failures. Your spiritual journey is not much different.

In short, you have to fail to move forward.

It's instinctive for us to want to pursue our purpose, and yet, many of us don't for the fear of failure. It makes us want to sit back and not leave our self-determined boundaries of safety.

It was that same fear that stopped me from being my true self at a young age. And because of these fears, I had come to regret a few decisions that I had made. Today, I can say with pride and happiness from my heart that I am grateful for the journey that I've had. So, take it from me or my experience – you have to push past the few uncomfortable roadblocks that are hiding your true self from you.

It's imperative that you don't let your ego or pride prevent you from pursuing your passions just because you failed once. I couldn't imagine the thought of where I would be now had I given up at the first sign of failure or discomfort.

Regardless of any outcome, there's always the lingering thought that should be present –

"I would rather try and fail than not try at all."

EMBRACING THE UNCOMFORTABLE

How many times have you wanted to do something only to back out and realize later that you should have just gone for it? It's your mind getting intimidated by the unknown and the uncomfortable things in life. It's our instinct to not escape outside its safety zone, but you have to understand that sometimes, it can hinder our potential for growth. After all, growth comes from the absorption and acceptance of new knowledge.

Embrace the fact that the uncomfortable is the key to progressing in life, in your spiritual journey and everything in between. It is only when we familiarize ourselves with what we are uncomfortable with that we can learn to be comfortable with them. And in doing so, we learn, grow, build character, and ultimately become more in touch with our true self.

Here are a few things I have used to embrace the uncomfortable.

SAY YES

Whenever the next opportunity for you to do something at school, work or in your daily life presents itself, simply say, yes.

Our minds, I've noticed, tend to take quite a liking to the comfortable. We thrive in it, actually. And because it makes our egos feel good, it becomes very easy for us to say no and remain comfortable than say yes to a potentially uncomfortable situation.

You never know when you will find something really interesting or worthwhile.

I'm sure there will be experiences that you might come to regret later as well, but learning to take everything in and using them for growth is also a part of the journey.

MAKE CHANGE

Your daily routine can say a lot about who you are, and your daily habits can say a lot about your ability to embrace the uncomfortable. I've seen it a million times – people going to work, getting settled in and then going brain dead for 8 hours. Running off of coffee, energy drinks, and auto-pilot.

Take some time in your day to write down all that you do. Then, begin to swap things out that are hindering your growth and/or add things to help. If you spend your whole lunch break sitting down after eating maybe try going for a quick walk. If you're close enough to work, try riding a bike instead of driving. I personally did this when I lived close to a previous workplace.

I would do about 11 miles round trip. It sucked at first and was wildly uncomfortable but slowly, I started getting more in shape and having more energy all the time. That allowed me to make other changes too. My coworkers joined in with me when I shared this with them, and then it became a fun activity that we could all do together. Had I just kept driving or carpooling to work, I would've never known that I would enjoy bicycling so much.

I also recommend that if you have a stressful work environment or tend to be stressed throughout the day, start with introducing meditation in your routine prior to leaving the house in the morning. You don't have to necessarily follow it to the mark, but mine went something like this for years.

- Wake up at 4-4:30 am.
- Express some gratitude.
- Meditate for 10-15 minutes.
- Then go about my usual routine before leaving to the gym or straight to work.

I would fall off schedule here and there, but I was also prepared for it. Habits don't happen overnight, so, I pressed on until it became easy. Change up your routine a little. You never know what will come out of it.

HESITATION MEANS JUMP

Right before doing something new, difficult, or uncomfortable, you may feel a slight hesitation. I'm not talking about the bad gut feeling hesitation but rather the anxious hesitation, almost like you know you should go after it but something in you isn't quite giving you the push.

Realize that sometimes, you just need to take a leap of faith and let nature run its course. What's meant to be will be – let that hesitation be your indicator that it is time to GO. Only look back when you truly feel against it from your gut.

You can't learn to swim if you're afraid of getting wet. You won't find your pure potential until you push to your limits using every failure as a means to boost yourself further. Every failure you will encounter brings you closer and closer to your goal, until you're eventually presented the opportunity for success.

Take the leap!

BACK ON TRACK

Some failures can seem small and controllable, while others may seem huge and out of our control. It's almost like watching your life get derailed and not being able to do anything about it. But the beautiful thing about life is that no matter where you go, you'll find new directions to explore and new things to learn.

Use that moment to close your eyes and reevaluate your position. Once you've done that, ask yourself if you want to keep heading in the same direction or take a different route. As long as you're willing to progress on with your journey, rest assured that your life is on the right track. It can't be helped that sometimes; we get sidetracked or take some wrong turns along our journeys. But these things won't matter as long as we keep heading towards our purpose. Any derailing, wrong turns, stopping at the wrong stations, or slow crossings you run into shouldn't stop you from keeping your train on course.

DIRECTION > SPEED

You are but a few failures away from being the person you've always wanted to be, and with every failure you encounter I hope you use them as stepping stones to build the future version of the self that you want to create.

You cannot change your past, so leave it there. The present is where a person is the happiest, so, enjoy it and you can change the future by the good you manifest right here in the present. Continue to give good unto the world and the world will continue to give good back to you. Even in the midst of turmoil, virtuous actions seldom go unnoticed.

Embrace the unknown, because you never know how many blessings are waiting for you and how much growth will come out of it. Stay on your path and stop worrying about how fast you'll get to any destination. Going in the right direction slow is better than hauling ass in the wrong direction.

8
HAVE TO MAINTAIN

You will continue to learn throughout your life and perhaps even beyond that. One significant lesson that I've learned so far on my journey is that more often than not, we are the ones hindering our own progress.

There's no need to think that you have to start at any particular point in your journey. The key is to simply begin. Start by becoming more aware and mindful of the present moment, and the rest will naturally follow. Trying to force or rush your progress by jumping into certain positions or actions will only hinder your journey and overall experience. Allow things to unfold naturally.

Remember, it's okay to make mistakes and encounter setbacks. In fact, they are an integral part of the learning process. Embrace the journey and stay open to new experiences and perspectives. By being present and accepting of what comes your way, you'll be better equipped to continue growing and evolving.

MAINTENANCE

Think of your spiritual journey and awareness like a flashlight. The brighter the light, the more present and aware you are, and the more consistently you practice. This allows you to see what's happening around you more clearly. Conversely, the less you practice and stay aware, the dimmer the light becomes, and the less you can see around you.

It seems that we often fall into cycles of complacency, fear, anxiety, depression, or valuing monetary gain above all else. These things can dim our inner light and darken the world around us. They also cloud our judgement, leading to poor decision-making.

That's why maintenance is key when embarking on a spiritual journey. By maintaining a regular practice of mindfulness and staying on our spiritual path, we become more focused and authentic. Finding what works for us and sticking with it is essential. I'll recommend trying out different methods to ensure you are doing everything you can to make the most of this human experience.

MY FAITH IS IN YOU

After reading this, my hope for you is that you will discover your purpose and strive to remain centered and true to yourself. May your relationships be plentiful and fulfilling, and may your mind become an unstoppable force. When life knocks you down, I hope that you will be quick to process and keep moving forward, thanks to the solid foundation you have built.

Don't forget to remind yourself of the progress you've made on your journey. It's easy to get caught up in the present moment and forget how far you've come. Remember that doubt and uncertainty are normal, but practicing gratitude can help you find perspective and maintain a positive outlook.

In difficult times, it's important to give thanks and appreciate the good in your life. Don't curse the rain if you took the sun's warmth for granted. Life is full of ups and downs, but by staying grounded and maintaining a sense of gratitude, you can weather any storm.

IF YOU CAN FALL, YOU CAN GET UP

Living and maintaining a spiritual journey can be both humbling and freeing, while at the same time, challenging and intimidating. Remember that you are never alone on this journey, and that like-minded individuals will align with you at some point. There is always room for growth and learning, so, continue to strengthen your foundation and create a processing palace that is abundant in space to process your traumas or troubles.

Find a routine that complements your lifestyle, or if necessary, make a new lifestyle that complements your new routine. Don't be afraid to try new practices or ideas because even in the worst-case scenario, you will be back to square one, and there's always room for improvement from there. Use the tools provided to discover yourself, become your biggest fan, and show the world how incredible it is to be yourself.

Also remember that failure is often a good indicator that you're getting closer to success. Keep jumping on those stepping stones, and keep your head up even in the midst of failure so you can see what needs to be learned in case there's a next time. Don't let failure overshadow your success; use your success to be the light in any form of darkness heading your way.

Finally, always remember – *if you can fall, you can get up*.

YOUR JOURNEY

I hope it brings you comfort to know that you are an essential part of this universe. Trust in your true self to guide you towards your highest potential and ultimate fulfillment. Detach from outcomes and stay focused on your purpose and intentions. The timing of things will be sorted out by the universe.

Let go of any fears or doubts and remain open to the endless love and wisdom of the universe. Continuously expressing gratitude for even the smallest things will manifest into greater things. As my mother used to say, "Take care of what you have now so God knows he can bless you with more." This philosophy can be applied to all aspects of life. Take care of your body now so future you is thankful for good health. Take care of your debts now so your future self is blessed with freedom. Take care of your spiritual journey now so your future self is blessed with peace and happiness.

Tending to and maintaining the things that matter most in your life in the present will lead to greater fulfillment in the future.

DIVE IN, JUMP OFF, TAKE THE LEAP

I was always told that taking a small step into a pond can create a big ripple, so imagine what a cannonball would do. To me, that meant that instead of hesitating towards a goal or task, I should go all in.

With everything in your life, just dive in, jump off the ledge, or take the leap. Bet on yourself and make sure to go all in.

I hope that with the tools provided and some patience, you can overcome everything in your way and always believe in yourself. Karson McGinley concludes a beautiful article on chopra.com with this quote:

> "If for whatever reason you're called to pursue a spiritual path, know that although the pathways vary, everyone is pointed in the same general direction."

So, whenever you start to feel like you're on a plateau or not progressing as fast as your peers, remember that everyone's journey is different, and yours is unique for a reason. Comparison will always be the thief of joy. Own your path, take pride in it, and remember that it's yours, and you make it just for you.

They are one and the same.

MY LEAVING THOUGHTS

I wish for peace, love, and happiness for all of you who have reached this point. It has been an honor that you have allowed me to be a part of your life, and I hope that wherever life takes you, you won't forget this little memory we shared.

For me, I believe this is just the beginning. I can talk a lot, so it was only a matter of time before I finally put some of my thoughts on paper. My social media links can be found on the about me page, so please feel free to reach out. I would love to read about people's spiritual journeys and how amazing we are as spiritual beings during our human experience.

Remember, you got this, you are worthy of being yourself and the world needs you to be, you.

I hope to see you in the next book.

Stay centered, friend.

ACKNOWLEDGMENTS

Getting my thoughts and feelings onto paper has always been a struggle so let this be an example to everyone thinking the same thing about themselves. If I can do it, so can you.

I would like to thank my wife Alex, who always supports me regardless of how emotionally (and financially) draining my dreams and desires can be sometimes.

To my beautiful mother, who never looked at any of my dreams as unfathomable, but rather gave me a get after it attitude. Your perseverance is inspiring. Now if we can just get you to write your book...

My beautiful sister, your critical analysis is probably the reason this book stayed alive and got me to keep pushing. Im grateful.

And to my dearest friends:

David Flores for your wisdom, making sure I'm not in my own way and keeping my head on straight when I'm overthinking.

Jarred Gunn for being honest and supportive at all times. You've seen me through all the highs and lows and never looked at me differently.

Fernando Villagran, my little brother from another mother, fate knew what it was doing when it brought us together, thank you for your never ending support and optimism even when its dark out.

Austin Moses, your tenacity and willingness to be uncomfortable, proves to everyone that keeping a smile and taking leaps in the moment of hesitation leads to progression.

Trevor Harden for being you. Your encouragement and support is always appreciated, especially your honesty.

Tyler Garner, your journey ended shorter than I think it was supposed to but, I know you're watching your brothers push the boundaries of what we thought was possible.

For our time, I am grateful. For your wisdom, I am grateful. For your brotherly presence and protective instinct, I am forever grateful and proud to call you my brother.

Where this book, or myself, would be without these people is far beyond me. All of you give me so much hope that I am living my life to my best potential and for that I'm thankful beyond measure.

About the Author

Chase is a Bakersfield, CA native with a career in video editing and music production. Growing up in the central valley, Chase developed a deep appreciation for art of all expressions. He discovered his love for poetry at 17, eventually leading him to venture into non-fiction writing. Chase draws inspiration from his life and experiences. *I Died So You Don't Have To* is his debut book, and he is currently working on his second.

Instagram - @chase.thewriter

References

[1] https://www.psychologytoday.com/us/blog/rediscovering-love/202108/dealing-defensive-walls

[2] https://psychcentral.com/health/the-masks-we-wear#causes

[3] https://theconversation.com/youre-not-crazy-recovery-from-trauma-is-different-for-everybody-41016

[4] https://www.goodreads.com/quotes/523350-if-you-are-depressed-you-are-living-in-the-past

[5] https://chopra.com/articles/the-correlation-between-spirituality-and-happiness